PRIMITIVE
BAPTIST
BELIEFS

(I Peter 3:15 and Jude 1:3)

2019

Jim Webb

TABLE OF CONTENTS

INTRODUCTION

"…and be ready always to give an answer to every man that asketh you a reason of the hope that is in you with meekness and fear:" (I Peter 3:15)

There are many "Christian" denominations of believers, and there are many variations of belief in all the denominations. It was not meant to be that way, but from the first generation of the church, there began to be false teachers and philosophies and divisions. Human nature, human reasoning, and human preferences have caused it. The result of these over two thousand years, has caused a wide variation of not only what is believed, but how people worship.

The problem of this result is that the purpose of worship has always been "to give praise and glory and honor to God." God is the only one who can judge if worship is acceptable to him. Men often judge by whether it feels and sounds good, whether it is inspirational in nature, if it draws numbers to the service, and if it seems civilized, educated, and reasonable. Whatever choices people make in their worship, they should be able to understand why they do things a particular way and why they believe in particular things. An example would be concerning the two men who went up to the temple to pray. Both were devout, but because of the difference in their worship, only one of them came away justified. God gave men a measuring stick when his son spoke to the woman at the well, that it must be "in spirit and in truth." In spirit does not just mean "with enthusiastic feelings" but means spiritually based rather than naturally based... pleasing to God rather than pleasing to man.

The purpose of this writing is to answer questions about the beliefs of one group of people (the Primitive Baptists) and the Bible reasons why they believe and practice the things they do. Included are many of the articles of faith of the Primitive Baptist Church. Descriptions and examples of these subjects have been drawn and gathered from many various writings and sources. They are not original with this writer or any one writer or source. Every reader is urged to read and study and pray for understanding of what is right and acceptable to God, and to understand the reasons and methods for the worship of their own church and to know if it is Biblical. Follow the instruction of the verse given at the beginning of this introduction. That means not only an answer, but with a humble attitude and a fear of God which is based on the desire to follow him both in spirit and truth.

WHAT'S IN A NAME?

What is a "Primitive Baptist?" "Disciples were called Christians first in Antioch." (Acts 11:26) At the time of that designation, it was meant to be a derogatory term. Through the centuries, Primitive Baptists have had many names, usually referring to a location or a particular belief or sometimes because of the name of a man who was prominent. However, for most of the time from the first century to the present, the Primitive Baptist Church had no particular name, and there is little or no written history of its existence. The reason was that it was highly persecuted and often worship had to be in hiding. Churches were independent and were often scattered and driven away. But the church clung to the teaching and practice of what was first taught and first delivered to the saints. The beliefs and teaching of what is now called Primitive Baptist, has existed since the days of the apostles. Historians have traced the believers of the early church, some were called Montanists up until about 150 AD, after which time some became known as Novations until about the time of the organization and beginning of the Catholic Church after 300 AD. Then some were called the Dontanists for more than a hundred years, and then for several centuries, more were known as Albigenses, and by 1100 AD some were known as Waldenses. All this time, there were many others not going by a name. They were hunted down and persecuted or put to death by whatever group had the most civil power at the time. At the time of the reformation, there were some

known as Anabaptists for not
accepting the baptisms of other
churches and requiring a second
baptism. Those who are now
Primitive Baptist were never
considered "protestant" because they
were never part of the Catholic church
in either belief or practice. Because of
huge differences in belief, they were
persecuted by the Catholic church
from its beginning through many
centuries. In their persecution while
being identified as anabaptists, often
death was by drowning and
laughingly referred to as a third
baptism by those who did it. The
general term of Baptist was first given
to a church name in the 1600's, but
thousands existed without a name
before that time. Many of the people
which became known as the Primitive
Baptists escaped Europe, England,
and Wales and came to America
beginning in the early eighteenth
century. In America they also were
called many names, such as
predestinarians, hardshells, particular

Baptists, and Old Baptists. By the early 1800's a large division occurred in what had become a large denomination in the early history of the colonies and the United States. The largest faction of the split adopted many practices and beliefs from protestant denominations, and the term Primitive Baptist was first used to take on the meaning of "original" Baptist. As with the word Christian, it was first used in a derogatory sense. These churches are now sometimes known as "Old School" Baptists, Old Baptists, Old-Line Baptists, and Predestinarian Baptists. Those who are now called Primitive Baptist have stayed with the fundamental doctrines first taught by the apostles, and the simple method of worship service like the early church, which only includes singing, praying, and preaching. The churches are independent, not run by a council or governing body. Their baptism is by immersion and for professed believers only.

The name Primitive Baptist means original Baptist, holding to the beliefs and practices of the church as was first set up by the apostles.

KING JAMES BIBLE

Why do Primitive Baptists use the King James Bible? When all the facts are considered, it might be more appropriate to ask why anyone would use any other translation. There have been hundreds of other translations, and the differences and departures from the King James translation are dramatic.

It should be understood that this is not just any book like other books. It is the Word of God. God has caused it to be written and breathed life into it and has protected and preserved it. The Bible writings, both the Old Testament and New Testament have been under attack with the intent to destroy it from the time it was written until now. But in the words of Jesus, it will continue to be preserved, "Heaven and earth shall pass away, but my words shall not pass away." (Matthew 24:35)

In a comparison to other translations, the KJV is from superior original text. There are two Hebrew basic texts of the Old Testament in existence. The one used in the KJV translation is called the Masoretic Hebrew text. It was unquestioned and used in all Bible translations until a second one began in the nineteenth century, which claimed that it was based on some older manuscripts. However, in its formation and use, it began to "correct" and change and omit words and phrases and then look for reasons to make changes. Some of the translations today are based on changes of Jerome, Josephus, Aquilla, the Samaritan Pentateuch and Theodotion to make unfounded corrections to a perfectly translated Hebrew text. In the Masoretic Hebrew text, there were eight strict rules that were followed by Hebrew scribes. These were to insure that each letter, word, and sentence of the Hebrew text was preserved exactly. One of the ways that God chose to preserve his words was to give total responsibility for the Old Testament to the Jews. "What advantage then hath the Jew? Or what profit is there of circumcision? Much every way: chiefly, because that unto them were committed the oracles of God." (Romans 3:1-2) The Jews kept and preserved the Hebrew Old Testament.

The KJV has superior New Testament Greek text. In the nineteenth century there were exhaustive studies of the exact and original words and in 1881 a work was commissioned called the English Revised Translation, which changed the original words in 5,604 places for a total of 9,970 words changed! New versions and translations (ERV, ASV, NIV, NASV, NKJV, RSV, NRSV,

TEV, JB, NEV, and more) since that time have followed the word changes that were started in the English Revised Translation. The changes made were almost universally accepted by educational institutions and seminaries. In existence today are more than 5,300 ancient manuscripts in cursive and hand print. In studying them, more than 99% of all wordings are in agreement with the Masoretic text and KJV translations, and less than 1% agree with changes made in the new translations. In addition, it has been shown that the variances in the other versions actually disagree with each other in hundreds of wordings in the four gospels alone. The omissions of words and phrases and the changing of words to sound more modern has dramatically changed meanings and understanding in hundreds of verses. For documentation and verification of what is said here, the reader is encouraged to look up the work of

D.A. Waite, in his book *Defending the King James Bible.*

A second reason that makes the KJV translation superior is the result of the men who did the translation and their system and rules in carrying out the translation. Fifty-four of the greatest scholars in the understanding and translation of these particular languages were chosen to begin the work in 1604. The work took seven years and forty-seven of the original translators continued to its completion in 1611. Not only were these men the most skilled in the languages and in their translating, but all were devout believers. They began and completed their work with the idea of translating exactly what was said rather than editing with a critical point of view. They divided into six groups of eight and each group took one section of the Bible and translated it and cross checked each other within their group. Then the groups exchanged their work with each other to further cross check until each group had checked and translated every part. It was such an exhaustive process that even with the world's greatest living scholars doing the work, it took seven years to its completion.

Another reason that the KJV Bible is more accurate is that it was translated by "verbal equivalence." That means that the very words are carried over from Hebrew or Greek to English. The word translate means "carry across." It does not mean change, add to, or subtract from. Nouns remain nouns, verbs remain verbs. However, in the more modern translations, "dynamic equivalence" is used. The word dynamic means "moving or changing." In a study between the KJV and the ASV, NKJV, and NIV translations, the NKJV had over 2,000 examples of dynamic equivalence. The ASV had more than 4,000 examples, and the NIV Bible had more than 6,600 examples of dynamic equivalence.

What those translations are doing is not translating, but paraphrasing. Here are several examples of dynamic equivalence to consider. First, in John 3:16, the words "should not perish" are taken out. This certainly causes a variation of the meaning of the verse. Another, in John 6:47 the words "on me" are removed from "He that believeth on me hath everlasting life." Does it matter what a person believes in? Another, in Romans 1:16, the words "of Christ" are removed from "For I am not ashamed of the gospel of Christ:" That opens the door for someone to believe anything that is called gospel. The three translations named above, the ASV, NKJV, and NIV, all follow this route. But multiply these three examples of dynamic equivalence times thousands to understand how much and how often it is done.

Some people have said that the KJV is old fashioned and outdated in its speech and needs to be more understandable by using the language that people talk in today. A study was actually done, using the KJV and the six other most used translations which mostly are written in more modern language. A computer program called "right writer" was used to measure the level of readability and ease of understanding of each one by plugging in the first chapter of every book of the Bible for each translation. Each translation was then given a score, a readability index, by the computer. The KJV had the best score and the NIV, which is the least accurate of the seven, was also much less readable as measured by the unbiased, educationally based computer program.

The Primitive Baptists believe by faith that the original Bible writers where inspired by God to pen the exact words and teachings which they wrote down. The importance of verbal equivalence in translation is paramount. Primitive Baptists also believe by faith that the King James translation was blessed and overseen by God, to be the exact truth and the most accurate and complete that has ever been written.

The first Primitive Baptist article of faith is this: "We believe that the scriptures comprising the Old and New Testaments, as given in what is known as the King James Translation, are of divine authority, and are to be taken as the only rule of faith and practice." The word by word inspiration of the scriptures is a fundamental point in Christian faith. If the scriptures are given merely by human authority, then the Christian structure is of human authority too, and would fail because Christianity is totally based on the scriptures.

Proof of the statement can only be arrived at by faith and through consideration of the evidence given in and about the scriptures themselves. The first of those proofs is the holy nature of the scripture. Its subject and descriptions are comprised of the things of God, lifting man up to a higher plain, showing the beauty of holiness and the perfection and unbounded wonder and attributes of God. The second of those proofs is its timeless perfection. No other book has ever matched its truths which apply to all generations since its writing. While books on every other subject written of by man must be updated regularly, this one stands firm as it was from the beginning. In spite of its opposition and enemies through the ages, none of it can be disproven. Only God could cause such a work to be done. Third, there is no other explanation for the fact that all the prophets have said has come true. So many hundreds of prophecies which were first written hundreds of years before their fulfillment all came true to the exact detail and none have ever been false. The most important of those are concerning the coming of Christ and his life.

Since these evidences show the characteristics of divine authority, and no other book known to man shows those marks, it is why the Primitive Baptists believe this is the "only" rule of faith and practice.

The Bible is given and meant to be "a lamp unto my feet, and a light unto my path" as David relates in the 119th Psalm. Paul describes its work and use in II Timothy: "for doctrine, for reproof, for correction, for instruction in righteousness: that the man of God may be perfect, throughly furnished unto all good works." The church is, by the scripture, given instruction to all church order and discipline as well as the description of the kind of preaching, praying, and singing which should be done in its service. Nothing is lacking. The scripture is also a complete guide for the individual as well as for the church.

THE TRINITY

The Primitive Baptists believe that there is one God, and that the Father, Son or Word, and the Holy Ghost are that one God, eternal, immutable, infinite in wisdom, power, justice, holiness, mercy and truth. Believing the Bible should make this declaration easy to accept. But even before there was a Bible, there were faithful men who believed these things. The Bible presents further evidence. The 19th Psalm begins with this statement, "The heavens declare the glory of God; and the firmament sheweth his handiwork." The harmony of all creation prove that these things could not have happened by chance. Only a God of infinite abilities could have designed it. The 90th Psalm further states, "Before the mountains were brought forth, or ever thou hadst formed the earth and the world, even from everlasting to everlasting, thou art God." The account of creation is given in the first chapters of Genesis, and the Primitive Baptists believe it just like it reads. While these things seem incredible to the human mind, it is because God is so superior to man that man cannot fathom such a power or wisdom. The tendency would be to try and explain things away by nature, but the truth is that if these things are not so, then the salvation of man is in jeopardy. With men many things are impossible, but with God all things are possible.

Only one being can be sovereign. So the conclusion is that there is only one God. There are many gods with a little g, but man has made those. The one with the big G created all things from nothing in six days. It is stated in Deuteronomy, "Know therefore this day, and consider it in thine heart, that the Lord he is God in heaven above, and upon the earth beneath: there is none else". Psalm 86 states "Thou art God alone." Paul says in I Corinthians 8:4 "There is none other God but one."

However, God has revealed himself to man in three ways. There are not three beings, but only one and that one has appeared to man three ways. "For there are three that bear record in heaven, the Father, the Word, and the Holy Ghost: and these three are one." (I John 5:7) The oneness of the trinity is a mystery, but it is clearly taught and illustrated throughout the Bible. "Without controversy great is the mystery of godliness: God was manifest in the flesh, justified in the Spirit, seen of angels, preached unto the Gentiles, believed on in the world, received up into glory." (I Timothy 3:16)

In the process of baptizing a believer, the Primitive Baptist minister says these or similar words, "upon the public profession of your faith, I baptize you my brother/sister in the name of the Father, the Son, and the Holy Ghost."

THE MUSIC

For someone attending a Primitive Baptist service for the first time, the very first impression might lead to the question "Why is there no instrumental music?" There is not a particular bias against instrumental music in general by those who attend the Primitive Baptist church. In fact the participants probably enjoy sacred instrumental music as much as anyone else. However, the music of the service is part of the worship service. The way to worship God the best in the church service is the way he has shown that is acceptable to him and the way that the church was set up from the beginning. There are two views concerning worship. The first is that people should only do what is instructed and exampled; the second is that people are free to do whatever is not forbidden. To use musical instruments would fall into the second category. To only use unaccompanied singing falls into the first category.

There are many references to singing in the New Testament church. There are no references to the use of instruments. Here are several which refer to singing:

"And that the Gentiles might glorify God for his mercy; as it is written, For this cause I will confess to thee among the Gentiles, and sing unto thy name." (Romans 15:9)

"What is it then? I will pray with the spirit, and I will pray with the understanding also: I will sing with the spirit, and I will sing with the understanding also." (I Corinthians 14:15)

"Speaking to yourselves in psalms and hymns and spiritual songs, singing and making melody in your heart to the Lord;" (Ephesians 5:19)

"Let the word of Christ dwell in you richly in all wisdom; teaching and admonishing one another in psalms and hymns and spiritual songs, singing with grace in your hearts to the Lord." (Colossians 3:16)

"Saying, I will declare thy name unto my brethren, in the midst of the church will I sing praise unto thee." (Hebrews 2:12)

"Is any among you afflicted? Let him pray. Is any merry? Let him sing psalms." (James 5:13)

These are biblical written instruction for singing in the New Testament worship service. There are no instructions or suggestions to play musical instruments in worship service.

Sometimes an argument is made that that the church does have in it things which were not in the first church such as electric lights and air conditioners and running water. These things may affect the worship setting but are not an integral part of the worship. Instrumental music would be an addition or change to the worship. In one sense, the music of the

Primitive Baptist is instrumental. The human voice is the musical instrument that every person is given by God at birth.

There are at least three reasons that musical instruments are not used in the Primitive Baptist worship services. The first one is that the scriptures are silent about it, which the church believes to be prohibitive rather than permissive. The second is that singing is something that is instructed for the participation of every worshiper. It is not a matter of whether a person has a musical gift but a spiritual gift to express what is in the heart. God hears what comes from the heart. The use of instruments or even choirs or soloists tends to cause the worshiper to be silent and listen (be passive) rather than participate (be active). The third reason is that all possible historical records and documents that have been found show that the early church did not use instrumental music. The earliest record of instrumental music in worship service was in the fourth century with organ music. Other instruments began to be used by the seventh century. The Primitive Baptist church is patterned to the early church as set up by the apostles.

THE MINISTRY

There are several questions to ask about the ministry. "Why aren't those aspiring to be Primitive Baptist ministers sent to seminaries or schools and trained?" Primitive Baptists believe that God calls ministers and puts on them a burden of preaching the gospel and being a pastor. This ability or gift is not something that someone can arbitrarily choose or go to school and become qualified for. It would probably be a "red flag" to any Primitive Baptist church if someone were "aspiring" to be a minister. The position of minister is not one of "power and influence" but one of a servant to the whole church body as well as to God to keep his house. A church recognizes the gift and has the individual speak and develop within the church. The preaching is to be a method of the duties of edifying, strengthening and comforting the church. Ministers are called from within a church and understand the makeup and circumstances of the church body and the foundations of truth which the church is formally built on. Formal education is unrelated to the call or gift. The church is admonished not to lay hands on someone suddenly, meaning before evidence and experience is sufficient. Members and other experienced ministers are expected to give encouragement and advice to one who is beginning. Some churches designate a person who is learning as "licensed" to practice while in a period of learning and being judged if there is a profitable gift. This practice, however, is not described in the Bible. At the time when a church believes the individual is ready to be a pastor, they call for the assistance of the ministry of nearby churches to organize a presbytery to question the church and the individual and then lay hands on the individual in a formal ordination. A minister remains under the care and discipline of the church of his membership. The ordination is not a ceremony which frees the minister to go wherever he wishes or choose his own path or field of labor. The church continues to be a judge in the preaching of the truth and in the exercise to edification and spiritual benefit.

"Why are there no women ministers in the Primitive Baptist church?" Both men and women fill a very important role in the church and in the home. Their teaching of children in the process of raising a family is a priceless and necessary gift. Women have an equal say in the voting rights in the business of the church and have much influence on the study and reading of the Bible in the home and in the participation of the church worship. However, in the example of the early church and the teaching of the epistles of Paul, women were not named or called to be ministers or deacons or for public speaking. These are simply not duties that the Bible appoints them to fill. There are many ways that a woman may minister to others, but there are no examples in the New Testament church of a woman being called to the preaching ministry. The Primitive Baptist church is patterned to the early church as set up by the apostles.

"Why are the ministry not salaried?" Salaried ministry would mean a business agreement where a minister would serve a church for a given period of time for a stipulated payment of money. This would be in direct conflict with Paul's teaching and example. "What is my reward then? Verily that, when I preach the gospel, I make the gospel of God without charge, that I abuse not my power in the gospel." (I Cor 9:18) A salaried system would bring into play such things as negotiating salary, pay raises, ambition of ministers to move to larger churches where the salary might be greater, and putting a financial burden on the persons being served. It could also sway the preacher to feel indebted to the congregation and make it more difficult to reprove, rebuke, or correct when it was necessary. These effects would be a definite corruption of the purposes, duties, and rewards of serving God's church as a minister. At most churches, people give donations through the church deacons which are meant to pay for church expenses and expenses or gratitude for the minister's travel and labors.

"Why are the ministers called 'elders' and why is the word 'reverend' or 'father' not used? The Bible gives the title elder to preachers. "The elders which are among you I exhort, who am also an elder…" (I Peter 5:1) The word reverend is not used for ministers because it is never used in connection with a man in the Bible. This title appears only once in the Bible and there it is a reference to God. "holy and reverend is his name" (Psalm 111:9) The Bible commands to call no man father. "And call no man your father upon the earth: for one is your Father, which is in heaven." (Matthew 23:9)

Primitive Baptists believe that those who give proof that they are called of God to the ministry, by edifying the church in that exercise, should be ordained by a presbytery and set apart to that work. Primitive Baptists believe that God calls ministers and gives them the burden of declaring the gospel. This is independent of anything that men can do. There is not only a call, but a gift or ability to understand the scriptures and declare them before the church in a way that will edify. It is a duty of the church to pray that God would send laborers into his harvest and then to watch for their appearance. The ordination is a formal recognition of the gift, but also is a way that a minister is still under the authority of the church. Jesus gave the first example of ordaining in Mark 3:14 "And he ordained twelve, that they should be with him, and that he might send them out to preach." Paul also speaks of it to Timothy in referring to the "laying on of the hands of the presbytery." The fourteenth chapter of Acts also refers to this service: "And when they had ordained them elders in every church." An ordination service is composed of the church and of ordained elders and deacons of other sister churches, who meet together to question and confirm the gift and calling and to lay hands on and approve of and pray for the one under consideration.

THE DEACONS

The Primitive Baptists believe that the church should choose properly qualified members for the office of deacon who are to receive and disburse the funds of the church. The deacon should be set apart to that work by ordination. The Greek word which is translated "deacon" means "servant, attendant, waiter." This is a special office of the church, especially meant for ministering to the needs of the body of the church in additional ways other than preaching. In the 6th chapter of Acts is recorded the first ordination of deacons. The church body had grown to a point that the apostles could not wait on (or minister to) everyone without giving up their preaching duties. They called together the church members and gave this instruction, "It is not reason that we should leave the word of God, and serve tables. Wherefore, brethren, look ye out among you seven men of honest report, full of the Holy Ghost and wisdom, whom we may appoint over this business." (Acts 6:2-3)

First of all, these verses point out the qualifications for the office. Secondly, the qualifications point to the duties to be carried out. These men are to be watchful for those in need and see to those needs with the resources of the church body. The actual deeds carried out covers a wide variety of things. In the church service, the deacon may be called on to serve communion. The deacons may decide the order of service. The deacon may be called on to offer prayer. The deacon may be called on to provide transportation of a member to meeting or to visit people who are sick or in the hospital. The deacon may be called on to visit someone who has been absent or who needs help or advice. The deacon may be called on to be the clerk of business meetings or the treasurer of the church and the one who pays the bills. The deacon may be one called on to make repairs to the church house or to make the church aware of coming expenses. The natural qualifications are that the person be honest and wise. The spiritual qualification is that he be full of the Holy Ghost. This means that he be able to treat people with spiritual understanding and with a humble, caring, and meek spirit.

BAPTISM

Primitive Baptists believe that baptism is by immersion in water and is to be administered only to those who have given evidence of spiritual life and professed their faith and belief in the finished work of Christ. It is to be administered only by one who has been properly ordained into the ministry. Baptism is one of the two ordinances of the church and baptism is the boundary line between the church and the world. Orderly baptism is required for membership in the Primitive Baptist church. Gospel baptism was first introduced by John the Baptist, announcing the coming of the Christ and the kingdom of heaven.

"Why do Primitive Baptists believe in baptism by immersion?" With certainly, every description of baptism in the New Testament is by immersion. Baptism is a symbolic act, signifying the death and burial and resurrection of Jesus. Burial has never been accomplished by sprinkling dirt over someone. They must be lowered into the grave. The idea of sprinkling came about for several reasons. One was that some churches believed that baptism was essential for eternal life. So those churches felt the need to baptize all possible people. That led to those who were sick or dying and unable to be baptized by immersion. Sprinkling and pouring were invented as methods that would accomplish salvation for someone who would go to hell without it. Because of a high infant death rate, that led to infant baptism becoming a regular practice.

Primitive Baptists believe that salvation was accomplished at the cross, and that baptism is the answer of a good conscience toward God of a person who is already saved. It is an act of faith and obedience rather than a condition to salvation. Baptism was by immersion from the time of the apostles until the practice of "pouring" began in the late third century. Infant baptism was also first practiced using immersion, but the first written papal law for pouring or sprinkling in the Catholic church was in the eighth century. There are no scriptures in the Bible which would authorize infant baptism, but only baptism of believers. When the Eunuch asked to be baptized, Philip answered "If thou believest with all thine heart, thou mayest. And he answered and said, I believe that Jesus Christ is the Son of God. And he commanded the chariot to stand still; and they went down both into the water, both Philip and the eunuch; and he baptized him. And when they were come up out of the water, the Spirit of the Lord caught away Philip," (Acts 8:36-39)

"Why do Primitive Baptists baptize someone over again who comes from another church?" Consider this: two couples get married and go through the ceremony and requirements and paperwork to make it legal. Then one spouse of each couple dies, and the remaining spouses decide to get married. Since they have both already accomplished a ceremony and paperwork of a marriage, should they be required to do it again? Of course they should, because they are making vows and commitment to a new person. Baptism brings a person into membership of a church and causes duties and obligations to that church. It is a public profession of devotion and intent to walk with and worship with the people, to fellowship, and to the beliefs of that church. A new ceremony is required, just as in the example of a new marriage. The ceremony and vows are not just to the belief in marriage in general, but to a new specific person (a new church).

Since baptism is not intended to give spiritual birth or eternal life, its purpose is for a believer to exercise his faith and commitment in a public way. Once again the example of marriage can be applied. Two people can live together without marriage, but marriage is the step which legally shows the love and commitment to each other. Baptism is an act which legally shows the love of a believer to God and his people and makes a public commitment to them. There is no authority given in the Bible for sprinkling, pouring, infant baptism, or church membership without baptism.

Should the Primitive Baptist church accept the baptism of an individual who by his/her previous baptism has professed faith in the principles and beliefs of some other denomination? Certainly not.

Primitive Baptists do not believe that it is acceptable for just anyone to administer baptism or for it to be done without the approval of the church. It is a responsibility of the ministry to baptize and to administer the communion. But it is the duty of the church to recognize the spiritual life of the one who has asked for it and to approve of the baptism into the membership of their body.

Primitive Baptists believe that there are three things necessary to proper Christian baptism. The first is a proper subject, whose heart has been touched by the grace of God and who desires to follow the Lord in a true gospel church way. The second is the mode, which is to be dipped or submerged in water. The third is a properly qualified minister, a man who is called of God to the work of the ministry and properly ordained by the church and currently in order and good standing with the church.

COMMUNION

Primitive Baptist churches observe the communion supper as one of their two church ordinances. It is to be practiced in memory of Christ and what he has done, until he comes again. There is a variance in how often it is observed, some churches doing it once a year, some twice, and others more. Primitive Baptists use unleavened bread and red wine for the emblems, which are symbols of the Lord's body and blood. Those were the exact items used in the original service. Only those who are members of the church and those who are in fellowship of like faith and order participate. The scripture gives several complete descriptions of exactly how the service is to be kept in Matthew 26, Mark 14, Luke 22, and I Corinthians 11.

"As they were eating, Jesus took bread, and blessed it, and brake it, and gave it to his disciples and said, Take, eat; This is my body. And he took the cup, and gave thanks, and gave it to them, saying Drink ye all of it; For this is my blood of the new testament, which is shed for many for the remission of sins." (Matthew 26:26-28) In the Primitive Baptist observance of it, the minister prays first, then breaks the bread, and then it is passed to the individual members. The minister pours the cup and prays again, and it is again passed individually to the members.

"Why do Primitive Baptists practice 'close' or 'closed' communion?" It is believed that this service is a church practice which is a memorial to what Christ has done and taught. Therefore, only those who have made a public profession of that in agreement with the beliefs and practices of the church are to participate. This is not a service with a purpose of imparting eternal life, but a memorial service that acknowledges Christ's perfect life, teaching, death, and resurrection. Participation not only applies the requirement of church membership, but that the church be at peace and in fellowship to be in a state to rightfully observe these things together. In addition, it is limited from participating with members of other churches who are not in agreement over either foundational beliefs or practices of church order and discipline. Jesus himself, in the first communion supper included only the apostles, telling them "Ye are they which have continued with me in my temptations." (Luke 22:28)

FOOTWASHING

The Primitive Baptists believe in and practice footwashing. It is not viewed as an ordinance but is viewed as a practice and example of service and humility that Jesus gave to the apostles, "If I then, your Lord and Master, have washed your feet; ye also ought to wash one another's feet." (John 13:14) The church observance of this practice is done at the time of the communion service. Just as communion is much more in meaning than just eating and drinking together, the meaning of this practice is deeper than only the literal washing of feet. It is a spiritual lesson to be observed spiritually between members at all times. While the communion ordinance shows what Jesus has done for his people, the footwashing service shows a necessary attitude, position, and relationship between people in the church which should cause a setting for proper worship and fellowship. The result is "If ye know these things, happy are ye if ye do them." (John 13:17)

MISSIONS

Shortly before his ascension, Christ commanded his apostles "go ye into all the world, and preach the gospel to every living creature." The Primitive Baptists do not interpret that this text was given to the church and that the church is now responsible for the spread of the gospel in the world today. The Primitive Baptists do not organize programs or raise funds for this purpose. Many denominations refer to this verse as "the great commission." However, it is not called that in the Bible. The apostles fulfilled this demand, and the apostle Paul states in Colossians 1:6 that the gospel has been preached unto all the world. And in Colossians 1:23 that it was preached to every creature under heaven. The apostles did that which Jesus commanded them and fulfilled it as he instructed. The idea that this verse of scripture was intended to be laid on the church instead of the apostles, is the doctrine which split the Baptist denomination in the early 1800's.

The terms mission and missionary do not appear in the Bible.

They represent the introduction of ideas which were advanced long after the scripture was written. Primitive Baptists do believe in ministers being led as directed by the Holy Spirit, but object to the idea that by missions eternal salvation is brought to individuals by the preaching of the gospel. The gospel does not cause eternal salvation, but reveals the salvation which God has already accomplished.

SUNDAY SCHOOL

The beginning of this tradition was in the eighteenth century, a move which used the Bible to teach children to read who lacked access to schools. While the intent was good, it turned into something else where the service of the church as set up by the apostles was changed or added to. A second issue comes into play, and that is that parents have an obligation in the home to read and teach the Bible to their children. When this is not done, the church will suffer. It is not the church's duty to do the parent's job. The culture of our country today is also suffering from this malady. Because parents do not teach or feed their children properly at home, the schools must take over many things that were not intended for the schools to be responsible for, until the education system becomes a social welfare system. A third factor is also important, and that is that the ministers are supposed to preach and teach the entire gospel so that all the congregation will be correctly schooled. The Primitive Baptist church does not support or practice Sunday school because it is not authorized in the Bible. This along with missions was a major point of disagreement in 1830 when the denomination had many split away from the Primitive Baptist original beliefs and practices.

A similar situation occurs with the subject of "Bible study." The words represent something good, and all Christians believe in reading and studying the Bible. Primitive Baptists do promote and encourage and believe in the importance of the reading and study of the Bible. But they do not support this activity replacing or being added to the service which was set up by the apostles. They also don't abandon that it is the duty of the parents to read and teach the Bible to their children and for the ministry to teach the Bible.

Primitive Baptists do not believe in innovations to the service or that any such practices would be an improvement over what was set in place by the apostles. Practices such as Sunday school and Bible study sound benevolent, but because they do not follow the Bible pattern, in a short time become a method of promoting heretical doctrines. Primitive Baptists believe in following the pattern of the church as it was set up by the apostles. The apostles were teaching fundamental doctrine to many beginners in the faith and there were always many children present. Even so, there are no examples of Sunday school, Bible study, or church camps in the New Testament.

HEAVEN AND HELL

Primitive Baptists believe in the resurrection of the dead, both of the just (elect) and the unjust, and that the unjust shall go away into everlasting punishment, but the righteous into life eternal. There are so many supporting scriptures for these, that it almost seems useless to make the point. However, the fact is that some people seem to feel wiser than the Bible words and teach doctrines contrary to it, or to simply think that parts of the Bible are not true.

The hope of the resurrection of all men is based on the resurrection of Christ, in which he overcame death as the last enemy to be defeated in his work here on earth. Death was the condemnation placed on all mankind after the sin of Adam. Until a perfect sacrifice could be made for sin, man would forever be subject to death. There are two ways to overcome death. One is by not dying, and the other is to revive back to life after dying. These two ways are described in I Thessalonians, chapter 4. Those who are dead will be raised to life, and those who are alive and remain will be caught up together with them in the clouds. For all his learning and effort, man has never found any way to prevent himself from dying. Even more impossible to believe is that men who are not able to prevent their own death while they were alive, could possibly regain their life from a dead state. By nature it is impossible. Even the believers and followers of Jesus did not believe he could do such a thing. But by the power of God, and the work of Christ, it became true. When the sacrifice of Christ (which required his death) was acceptable as a perfect sacrifice to God, he raised up to life again that body that had died, in victory over death. Why is that meaningful to anyone else? It is because he did not die or rise to life again to save himself, but he came to save those who were lost because of the law of sin and death. "For I came down from heaven, not to do mine own will, but the will of him that sent me. And this is the Father's will which hath sent me, that of all which he hath given me I should lose nothing, but should raise it up again at the last day." (John 6:38-39)

That there will be a resurrection of both the just and unjust is plainly stated in the Bible. "…that there shall be a resurrection of the dead, both of the just and the unjust." (Acts 24:15) Further, in the words of Jesus himself, "Marvel not at this: for the hour is coming in the which all that are in the graves shall hear his voice, and shall come forth; they that have done good, unto the resurrection of life; and they that have done evil unto the resurrection of damnation." (John 5:28-29) And again, by Daniel, "And many of them that sleep in the dust of the earth shall awake, some to everlasting life, and some to shame and everlasting contempt." (Daniel 12:2) Paul did not rejoice just in the fact that Jesus had defeated sin, but he rejoiced in the meaning for the elect: "Thanks be to God which giveth us the victory through our Lord Jesus Christ." (I Corinthians 15:57)

The Primitive Baptists believe that these same bodies which have died will be resurrected. But they will be changed and made fit for eternal heaven where sin cannot enter. "Behold I shew you a mystery; we shall not all sleep, but we shall all be changed, in a moment, in the twinkling of an eye, at the last trump:

for the trumpet shall sound, and the dead shall be raised incorruptible, and we shall be changed." (I Corinthians 15:51-52) The human body that here is sinful and corruptible will be changed into one that is incorruptible. It is the same body as the one that died. If it was any other body, it would not be a resurrection but a substitution. And it is not the soul (spirit) which is resurrected, because it did not die. At the time of the death of the body, the soul went back to God who gave it. At the time of the resurrection, the soul and body are joined together again in a changed state and are bound for glory.

Now the first point is that all who have lived on earth will be resurrected on the judgment day. But the next point is that they will be separated into two groups, which these listed scriptures have pointed out. "Then shall the King say unto them on his right hand, Come, ye blessed of my Father, inherit the kingdom prepared for you from the foundation of the world. Then shall he say also unto them on the left hand Depart from me ye cursed, into everlasting fire, prepared for the devil and his angels." (Matthew 25:34) It is very obvious that there are two places.

Is there a heaven? Turn to the book of Revelation and chapters 21 and 22. There is a description not only of what heaven is like in its glory and beauty, but it also lists the many things that will not be there. No more death, sorrow, crying, pain, no sun or moon, no curse of sin, and no night there. The glory of God will lighten it and the Lamb will be the light thereof.

That description is a fitting one in the book that the children of God need here in this world. It is to be a place where there will be no bad, no evil, and no ending. Chapter 21 ends by telling who it is that will live there: "they which are written in the Lamb's book of life."

However, in chapter 20 is the answer to the question "Is there a hell?" A comment was overheard, by someone discussing the subject, after one person said they didn't believe in it. God wouldn't do that to anyone. The other one answered, "you won't be there five minutes before you will change your mind." Of course they were joking with each other, but it is a serious subject. The first of those who will be housed in hell are Satan and his angels. A description of it is given, but those who love God need to keep their focus only on heaven. The rest of those who the Bible says will join Satan and his angels are "And whosoever was not found written in the book of life was cast into the lake of fire." (Revelation 20:15)

ELECTION

Primitive Baptists believe that God chose a definite number of particular persons to salvation before the world was formed. Some people have believed that God was able to do this because he looked ahead in time and knew who would do good and who would believe in him. Here are some Bible statements at different points in time: "God saw that the wickedness of man was great in the earth, and every imagination of the thoughts of his heart, was only evil continually." (Genesis 6:5) This was 2,500 years before Christ. "The Lord looked down from heaven upon the children of men to see if there were any that did understand and seek God. They are all gone aside, they are all together become filthy; there is none that doeth good, no, not one." (Psalms 14:2-3) This was 1,500 years before Christ. "There is none that understandeth, there is none that seeketh after God, they are all gone out of the way, they are together become unprofitable; there is none that doeth good, no, not one." (Romans 3:11-12) This was 30 years after the crucifixion of Christ. It would be difficult to believe that there were any elect at all if God determined the worthiness of men by their works. All from the beginning of time to the first generation of the church had failed.

God does make a point of how his election works and does not work. "For the children being not yet born, neither having done any good or evil, that the purpose of God according to election might stand, not of works, but of him that calleth." Romans 9:11) Further texts which clearly state election and its time can be found. "According as he hath chosen us in him before the foundation of the world, that we should be holy and without blame before him in love: having predestinated us unto the adoption of children by Jesus Christ to himself, according to the good pleasure of his will." (Ephesians 1:4-5) "Who hath saved us, and called us with a holy calling, not according to our works, but according to his own purpose and grace, which was given us in Christ Jesus before the world began," (II Timothy 1:9) It is obvious that election happened before the creation of the world, and that it was not based on any works of men.

The doctrine of God's election leaves the non-elect right where any conditional system leaves all mankind, to their own will and to their own works.

"No man can come to me except the Father who sent me draw him, and I will raise him up at the last day." (John 6:44) The natural man is not drawn to God. It is a great blessing that God has drawn the elect to himself. "Blessed is the man whom thou choosest, and causest to approach unto thee." (Psalm 65:4) and "I have loved thee with an everlasting love: therefore with loving kindness have I drawn thee." (Jeremiah 31:3)

"Are Primitive Baptists Calvinists?" In ancient days, the Jews looked at all people and categorized them as Jew or Gentile. In modern days, some tend to do the same in religious circles, categorizing all as either Arminians (those who advocate the teaching of James Arminius) or Calvinists (those who advocate the teaching of John Calvin). When people see that the Primitive Baptist believe in election and predestination, they sometimes think that Primitive Baptists are a branch of the Calvinist beliefs. However, they have never been and there are significant differences between them.

Primitive Baptists are not protestants but have been in existence since the days of the apostles. Calvin was a protestant reformer, formerly a Catholic, and the founder of what became the Presbyterian church. Calvin taught that the elect would persevere, but if someone did not, it proved they were not of the elect. So salvation depended on their ability to persevere. The Primitive Baptists believe that final perseverance of the elect is of God, not because of man's faithfulness, and that none of the elect can be lost. A child may fall from his own faithfulness, but never from God's covenant favor. Calvin believed in double predestination, that by predestinating some to heaven, God also predestined everyone else to hell. Primitive Baptists believe God has predestined the elect to heaven, and that the non-elect are simply left in their fallen state. Calvin taught absolute predestination, that God caused all "things" to be as they are. Primitive Baptists believe that predestination only refers to the final destiny of God's people. Calvin believed in and practiced infant baptism. Primitive Baptists believe that all people, no matter what age, are saved the same way, by grace alone. Calvin was also involved in the persecution of those who disagreed with his teaching, which made him no better than the Catholics who persecuted the protestants. The

Primitive Baptists have never persecuted any. No, the Primitive Baptists are not Calvinists.

PREDESTINATION

Primitive Baptists believe that God has predestinated the elect unto the adoption of children by Jesus Christ according to the good pleasure of his will.

The word predestination is not found in the Bible. The word predestinate is found twice in the book of Romans and the word predestinated is found twice in the book of Ephesians. The word predestination refers to the doctrine that God pre-established the eternal destiny of the elect. Sometimes a reader has been confused to think that God predestined because of his foreknowledge. In the 8th chapter of Romans, the works of God are listed, beginning this way, "For whom he did foreknow, he also did predestinate to be conformed to the image of his Son, that he might be the firstborn among many brethren." A point is made here that predestination is of persons, not of things or events. If predestination were done because of knowledge of the works and decisions of men, then the scripture would have begun with the words "For 'what' he did foreknow" instead of "For "whom' he did foreknow." The same logic applies to Ephesians 1:5, "Having predestinated us to the adoption of children by Jesus Christ to himself, according to the good pleasure of his will." It is speaking of people, not events. It would be inappropriate to say "Having predestinated 'all things' to the adoption of children" which makes no sense at all. Events cannot be children.

Further truth concerning predestination is that it in no way depends on the belief of men. The destiny of the elect of God is eternally fixed. It cannot be changed or lost. Nothing can separate the elect from the love of God.

"Do Primitive Baptists believe what is to be will be? Do we believe that God has set a time when each person will die?" Primitive Baptists do not believe that God predestined all events. But he has accomplished all the things necessary to achieve his purposes. The Bible has given many prophecies, and for sure every one either has come true or will come true.

In the book of Ecclesiastes, it tells that for everything there is a season and there is a time for everything. It is saying that there is an appropriate time for all things. Crops are to be planted in the spring and harvested in the fall. It wouldn't work to plant most things in the fall or winter. God is not responsible for all the terrible things that happen on earth, but they have come about because of men and sin. When someone dies in an accident or has cancer, God did not cause that. God set this creation up a certain way, and man can't do anything about it and must live with the way God made it. Man cannot decide that he won't abide by the law of gravity or change how fast the world turns or by eating right live to be five hundred years old.

God's purposes will come about. Men will be happiest and most blessed if they conform their wishes to God's will and purpose.

JOHN 3:16

"For God so loved the world, that he gave his only begotten Son, that whosoever believeth in him should not perish, but have everlasting life."

The first half of this chapter is devoted to a conversation and lesson with Nicodemus and about being born again. Many of the lessons in the book of John are about the change that must take place from the natural to the spiritual or a contrast between them.

The word world is derived from the root word kosmos, which means a particular order of persons. When there is more than one order of persons, there is more than one world. The key to this verse is "what world" is Jesus speaking of. The word world here is the same world as in I John 2:2 "And he is the propitiation for our sins; and not for ours only, but also for the sins of the whole world." This means the world that God loved. Esau could not belong to that world because it is written "Esau have I hated." Jacob did not belong to the same world as Esau because God said "Jacob have I loved." The world of John 3:16 and I John 2:2 is the world of the elect. In John 17:9, Jesus said, "I pray not for the world, but for them which thou hast given me, for they are thine." Here the world of the non-elect is referred to. So there was more than one world, and he prayed for the elect world which God loved. Again Jesus said "all mine are thine, and thine are mine; and I am glorified in them" in John 17:10. Jesus is glorified in every one born of the elect world. God loved the elect world so much that he gave his only begotten son for them.

"Whosoever believeth" is not a condition to be met to obtain eternal life. "He that heareth my word, and believeth on him that sent me, hath everlasting life." (John 5:24) Emphasize it says "hath" not "will have." And "Whosoever believeth that Jesus is the Christ is born of God" (I John 5:1) Emphasize it says "is" not "will be." "My sheep hear my voice, and I know them, and they follow me: And I give unto them eternal life; and they shall never perish, neither shall any man pluck them out of my hand." (John 10:27-28) Emphasize the word "my" which refers to the elect, those who are already his. If God had loved everyone so much that he sent Jesus to die for them all, all of them would be the elect and none would be lost. This is why it is certain that Jesus died for only the elect world. Not everyone is elect, example: Esau.

Jesus was speaking with Nicodemus, who was a Pharisee and a ruler of the Jews. From a Jewish point of view, God's promises were to the Jews, the descendants of Abraham. Part of the lesson is to explain that God also has a people among the Gentiles. National Israel is a small country, but spiritual Israel is like the stars of heaven or sands of the sea. Spiritual Israel is made up of those who are born again of the Spirit.

ROMANS 10:9

"That if thou shalt confess with thy mouth the Lord Jesus, and shalt believe in thine heart that God hath raised him from the dead, thou shalt be saved."

One of the most common reasons for misunderstanding scripture is taking a verse or phrase out of its context. Paul is writing this letter to the Church and the saints at Rome, not to save souls but to establish the foundational doctrines to the church there. He was writing to believers. Who can confess with the mouth and believe with the heart that Jesus is the Christ? Only one who is already born of the Spirit. Does confessing Christ cause salvation? Does believing in Christ cause salvation? These are not the cause of salvation, but the evidence of salvation. Salvation was completely accomplished at the cross. One of the strong wishes of Paul was that the saints might know of their salvation. "Therefore I endure all things for the elect's sakes, that they may also obtain the salvation which is in Christ

Jesus with eternal glory." (II Timothy 2:8-10) The elect do not have to do anything to accomplish salvation. By obtain, Paul means "embrace it." Their faithfulness and understanding, and their confession and belief can make their election seem more sure to them. It is already sure to God. Doubts and fears about salvation will arise if they do not understand truthfully the great works that God has done on their behalf. Exercising their faith in the righteousness of God will "save" them from those doubts and fears about their own lack of righteousness. These are the thoughts leading up to the 9th verse. And this is the meaning of Paul beginning that chapter with the desire that they might be "saved" when he is addressing those who are already believers in the church. In this chapter, Paul continues by speaking of God's calling, teaching, and sending the gospel according to his own will.

REVELATION 3:20-22

"Behold, I stand at the door, and knock: if any man hear my voice, and open the door, I will come in to him, and will sup with him, and he with me. To him that overcometh will I grant to sit with me in my throne, even as I also overcame, and am set down with my Father in his throne. He that hath an ear, let him hear what the Spirit saith unto the churches."

There is no such thing as Jesus standing at the door of a dead and alien sinner's heart, begging for entrance; and if the sinner will open the door, Jesus will come in and the sinner be saved. This scripture is addressed to a church, the Church of Laodicea. This church had been blessed of natural things and had become luke-warm spiritually. They thought they were rich because of natural things, but they were poor by not seeing the value of spiritual things. For the church to be truly blessed it must approach the Lord's throne and sit down at the Lord's table and partake of spiritual things and worship together with Christ.

REVELATION 22:17

"And the Spirit and the bride say, come. And let him that heareth say, Come. And let him that is athirst come. And whosoever will, let him take the water of life freely."

Some persons have read this to mean that someone who is not saved can become saved by deciding to partake of spiritual things. The first point is that the Bible is written and addressed to those who are saved, those who are God's children already. The second point is that the natural man is not drawn to spiritual things. He is dead to them. "No man can come to me, except the Father which hath sent me draw him: and I will raise him up at the last day." This is not an invitation to accept salvation, but is instruction for the child of God to enjoy that salvation that God has provided for him.

The Holy Ghost (the Spirit) and the church (the bride) urge the members to obedience and service and a life of faith and grace. Those who are obedient to the drawing of the Spirit do come and join in with it and the church. Jesus said, "blessed are they that hunger and thirst after righteousness: for they shall be filled." Only those who have spiritual life hunger and thirst after spiritual things. When they do, they will be fed. There are things which money cannot buy, that are without price. There is no price a sinner can pay to purchase salvation. It has already been paid for. But one who is born spiritually may get much refreshment and strength when they partake of it. The reason this instruction is given is because many who have salvation are not obedient and do not partake of its blessings as they should.

ARTICLES OF FAITH

In the more recent centuries of history, each Primitive Baptist church has written out its own "articles of faith" which establish the beliefs based only on the Bible. Wordings may vary from church to church. This is a representative list that would fit the beliefs of the original Primitive Baptist churches as believed and practiced from the time of the apostles to the present.

We believe that the scriptures comprising the Old and New Testaments, as given in what is known as the King James Translation, are of divine authority, and are to be taken as the only rule of faith and practice. (Deuteronomy 4:2, Hebrews 1:1-2, Romans 15:4, II Timothy 3:15-16, Luke 1:3-4, Revelation 22:18-19)

We believe in one God, and
that the Father, Son or Word, and the
holy Ghost are one God, eternal,
immutable, infinite in wisdom, power,
justice, holiness, mercy and truth.
(Deuteronomy 6:4, Jeremiah 10:10, I
Corinthians 8:6, I Timothy 2:5, I
Timothy 1:17, I John 5:7, John 1:1,
John 10:30, Matthew 28:19)

We believe that in the
transgression of Adam he fell under
the condemnation of God's holy law,
and that all his posterity were
corrupted in him, and so are
condemned in sin, and have neither
will nor power to deliver themselves
from this state of condemnation.
(Genesis 2:17, Romans 5:12-19,
Romans 3:9-23, Romans 8:7,
Ephesians 2:1)

We believe that God chose a
definite number of particular persons
of the fallen posterity of Adam in
Christ before the foundation of the
world to salvation. The reason for this
choice is wholly of grace and is

unconditional on the part of the creature. (Ephesians 1:4, I Thessalonians 1:4, Romans 9:11, II Thessalonians 2:13, I Peter 1:2, II Timothy 2:19, Ephesians 2:4-9, Revelation 13:8)

We believe that God has predestinated the elect unto the adoption of children by Jesus Christ according to the good pleasure of his will. (Ephesians 1:5, Romans 8:29, Ephesians 3:11)

We believe that the Lord Jesus who was set up from everlasting to be the mediator between God and men, did in the fullness of time really and truly take upon himself a human body and nature, sin excepted, and in that body he suffered, bled and died as the surety of the elect, and in their room and stead, and for no others. (Hebrews 7:15-16, Hebrews 8:3, Galatians 4:4-5, Hebrews 10:5-10, John 17:9)

We believe that Christ hath obtained eternal redemption for the elect, his life, suffering, blood and death constituting a complete and full atonement for their sins, and that this is the only ground of justification before God. (Isaiah 53:5, Hebrews 9:26-28, Hebrews 9:12, Hebrews 10:14, Ephesians 1:7)

We believe that being born again is not the act of man, nor dies it result from what he may believe or do; but it is the work of God, who gives eternal life, thus quickening the sinner, which causes him to confess his sin, and to feel the need of a Saviour. (John 3:3, John 1:18, John 5:21-25, John 10:28, II Timothy1:9, Ephesians 2:1-5)

We believe that none who are born again will fall away so as to be eternally lost, but that they will persevere through grace to glory. (John 10:28-29, John 6:39-44, I Peter 1:5-23, Romans 8:30, Jeremiah 32:40)

We believe in the resurrection of the dead, both of the just (elect) and the unjust, and that the unjust shall go away into everlasting punishment, but the righteous into life eternal. (I Corinthians 15:4-52, I Thessalonians 4:14, Daniel 12:2, II Thessalonians 1:8-9, Matthew 25:34-46)

We believe that the gospel is to be preached in all the world as a statement of the truth, and as a witness of Jesus for the comfort and instruction of regenerated men and women; but deny that it is to offer grace to the unregenerate or that it asserts there is an obligation resting upon the unregenerate to believe that Jesus is their Saviour. (Matthew 24:14, Mark 15:16, Acts 13:48, Romans 1:16, II Timothy 3:16-17)

We believe that good works, obedience to the commands of God, are well pleasing in his sight, and should be maintained in the church; but they are to be considered only as evidence of a gracious state and are not a condition of salvation. (Matthew 5:16, Luke 17:10, Ephesians 2:8-10, Titus 3:8, Hebrews 10:24)

We believe that baptism and the Lord's Supper are ordinances appointed by Christ for the church, and they are to be administered only by those who are clothed with authority of the church, having been regularly ordained. (Matthew 28:19, Luke 22:19-20)

We believe that baptism is by immersion in water and is to be administered to believers only, and who give evidence of having been regenerated. (Matthew 3:16, John 3:23, Acts 8:37-39, Romans 6:4)

We believe that the Lord's Supper should be observed in the church until the coming of Jesus at the end of the world, and that unleavened bread and wine should be used, of which none are to be invited to partake but members of the church and of other churches of like faith and order and fellowship. (Matthew 26:17-27, Exodus 13:7)

We believe that washing the saints' feet is an example of Jesus Christ to be observed by the church. (John 13:4-15)

We believe that those who give proof that they are called of God to the ministry, by edifying the church in that exercise, should be ordained by a presbytery and set apart to that work. (Mark 3:14, Acts 14:23, I Timothy 2:7, I Timothy 4:14)

We believe that the church should choose members of its body who have the proper qualifications for the office of deacon and that they should be set apart for that work by ordination. (Acts 6:3-6, I Timothy 3:8-13)

RULES OF DECORUM

In the more recent centuries of history, each Primitive Baptist church has written out its own "rules of decorum" which establish the meeting times, the order of business, the appointment of a moderator, and how business is to be conducted and a record kept. It defines the order that is to be followed in member speaking and voting and the method that will be followed when there are offenses. These are individually written and adopted by churches and can vary from church to church. They are meant to give structure, order, and respect to the process of church business. These rules may be amended at any time that the church sees a need for it.

A sample of the order of business would be: invite visiting brethren to seats in council, announce the opportunity for persons to unite with the church, call for reference from previous meetings, take up matters concerning fellowship, introduce new business, read and approve minutes which will become a legal record of the church meeting and business.

CONCLUSION

"...it was needful for me to write unto you, and exhort you that ye should earnestly contend for the faith which was once delivered to the saints." (Jude 1:3)

It seems a sad thing that there are so many divisions and systems of religion and worship now. Even in most denominations, and in those called by the Primitive Baptist name, there are disagreements and departures from what was first delivered to the saints. One cannot believe that God is pleased at this, or that people will be blessed as much as if they held to the service and worship as it was set up and first given by the apostles. However, reading this verse is evidence that false doctrines, false teachers, and divisions were already present and a threat to the church in the first century. Jude started out to write about a grand subject, and then realized it was more important to give this warning, so that the church as originally set up would be preserved until Christ's return. Our thanksgiving is because of those who through the ages have labored, suffered, and been faithful and that there is still a remnant who hold to the beliefs, practice, and discipline as it was first delivered.

CPSIA information can be obtained
at www.ICGtesting.com
Printed in the USA
LVHW050758060520
655002LV00002B/362